The Joke's On Ewe

by BFFs
Annie Thiel and Mary Hirsch

Annie and Mary dedicate
this book to their
families and friends.

Published by Mary E. Hirsch
in the United States

www.swellgals.com

First Edition

A portion of the sales of this book
benefit Special Olympics

Q: **What do you call twin witches?**

A: Twitches.

Q: **What kind of bug does a lot of walking?**

A: A shoe-fly.

Q: **What do sea turtles have for lunch?**

A: A peanut butter and jellyfish sandwich.

*   *   *

1

Q: Where does a bat go for a little privacy?

A: To the bat room.

Q: Where do baby ghosts sit?

A: In a boo-ster seat.

Q: When is a soccer player like a state?

A: When she's wearing a New Jersey.

* * *

Q: Why don't you want to make an octopus mad?

A: Because when he's up in arms, he's really up in arms!!!!!

Q: Where do chimps like to go to hang out with their friends?

.A: A monkey bar.

Q: Why did the cow build a rocket ship?

A: She wanted to visit the Milky Way.

Q: Why do chickens have feathers?

A: They don't want to run around the farm naked.

Q: What do you say to an optometrist?

A: I have eyes for you.

Q: Where does a police officer go for a good meal?

A: A steak out.

*   *   *

4

Q: **What is very old and made of silver?**

A: A dimeasaur.

Q: **What food watches the most television?**

A: A couch potato.

Q: **What's the best time to go to a dentist?**

A: Tooth thirty.

Q: **What did the teacher say to the kids at the circus?**

A: Start clowning around.

Q: **What does a judge really want when she says "order in the court"?**

A: A cheeseburger and French fries.

Q: **What do reptiles use to clean their cars?**

A: Turtle wax.

Q: **Why is Cinderella such a great basketball player?**

A: She likes to go to the ball.

Q: **Why does thunder like to hang out at the bowling alley?**

A: It likes to strike.

Q: **What does a lawyer say to someone when he's leaving?**

A: I'll sue you later.

Q: What first word does a baby website say?

A: Goo-Google.

Q: What is a golfer's favorite number?

A: Four.

Q: Why was the owl ghost so sad?

A: It could only say Boo Who.

Q: What animal can't you trust?

A: A cheetah.

*   *   *

Q: What kind of test do they give at Coca-Cola University?

A: A pop quiz.

Q: What kind of a treat does Santa like to eat?

A: Ho-Hos.

Q: If you are hungry at the playground where should you go?

A: To the sand-wich box.

* * *

Q: What kind of juice do people wearing lots of diamonds like to drink?

A: Karat Juice.

Q: Where do dogs park their car?

A: In a barking lot.

Q: Why can't an octopus drive a car?

A: He doesn't have a driver's license -- DUH!!

Q: What is white and explores the world?

A: Marco Polar Bear.

Q: The Smiths have three children. The oldest is Will, the youngest is Jill and the other is Dill. Why did they name him Dill?

A: They wanted a pickle in the middle.

Q: What do you call an antique clock?

A: An old timer.

*   *   *

11

Q: What kind of drink does a cry baby like?

A: Whine.

Q: Why did the doctor want to put the sun in the hospital?

A: It's always running a fever.

Q: What does Michelle Obama like to collect?

A: Sea Mi-shells.

Q: What is blue and spends a lot of time in front of a computer?

A: A web Smurf-er.

Q: How do goblins stay so sad?

A: Good glooming.

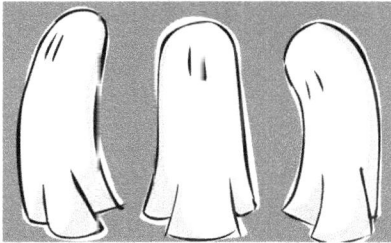

Q: How does a snail make you laugh?

A: It tells you a slow poke joke.

Q: Why did the witches go to the hobby store?

A: They wanted to make witch crafts.

Q: **What do you say when you hire a new fire fighter?**

A: You're fired.

Q: **How do you hunt for clouds?**

A: With a rain bow and arrow.

Q: **What kind of test does mascara take?**

A: A make-up quiz.

Q: What kind of candy does a shark like to eat?

A: A jaws breaker.

Q: What did the vowels say to the Mississippi?

A: I only have "I"s for you!!.

Q: What do you say when you pull a trick on a sheep?

A: The jokes on ewe.

*   *   *

Q: **Why was the egg acting so silly?**

A: It had cracked up.

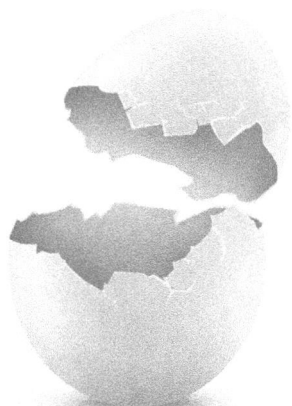

Q: **Why was Freddy washing his trampoline?**

A: His mom said it was time for spring cleaning.

Q: **What do geese get when they read a mystery?**

A: Peoplebumps.

Q: **Where do spiders find dates?**

A: On a dating web-site.

Q: **Why did the watermelons have a big wedding?**

A: Because they can't-elope.

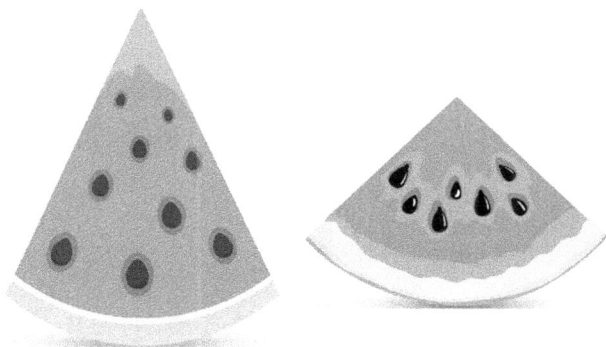

Q: **What kind of dance do arms and legs do?**

A: They like to limb-bo.

Q: Where do apes go to workout?

A: The jungle gym.

Q: What food does a basketball player hate?

A: Turnovers.

Q: What do you call a strong cloud?

A: A super soaker.

*   *   *

Q: Who is the best bowler on a farm?

A: A turkey.

Q: What's the best way to take a picture of a swimmer?

A: With a Poolaroid camera.

Q: What do comedian chickens say?

A: "The yolks on you."

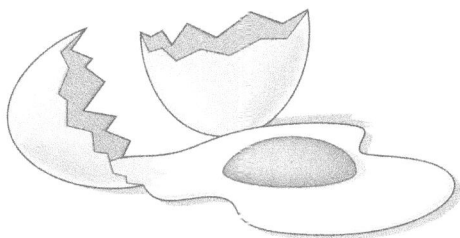

Q: Where do pebbles like to cut loose?

A: At a rock concert.

Q: What do spiders like to eat at picnics?

A: Corn on the cobweb.

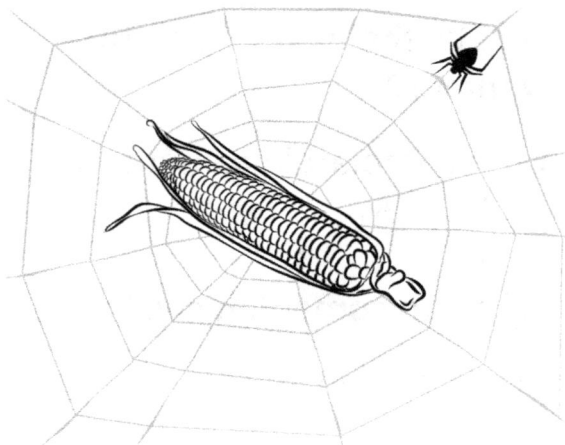

Q: What is the favorite game to play in the swamp?

A: Leap frog.

Q: Why did the bird want another beer?

A: It's a Tu-can bird.

*   *   *

Q: Why is there a giraffe on the last page?

A: So we can say "so long."

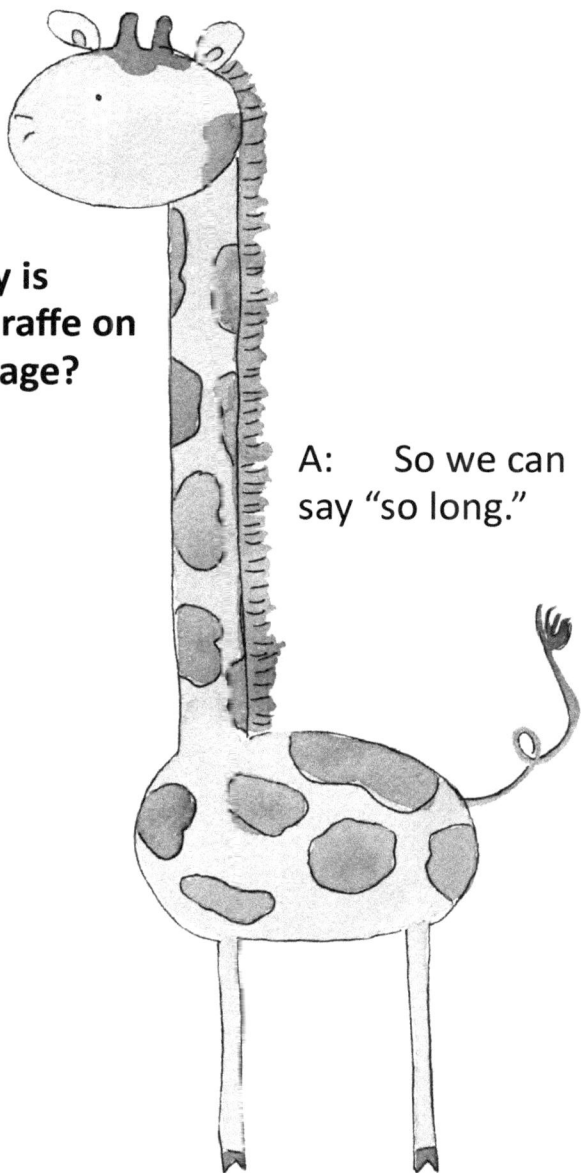

About The Authors

Annie and Mary met in 2003 when they were working at the same law firm. They became instant pals and it wasn't long before they were hanging out as BFFs.

Annie is an Uno card shark and a Scrabble genius. She has been active in the Special Olympics doing swimming, bowling, and track -- track is her favorite. She has won a lot of medals and ribbons over the years. Annie also loves to go to movies, concerts, ride her bike, hang out with her cousins, and, of course, make-up jokes.

Mary loves to play Uno and Scrabble with Annie, although she does not win at Uno too often. She works as a marketing manager but also is a writer, humorist, comedian, and swell gal. Mary hangs out with her beagle, rides around in her 1999 red Cabrio Bessie, and is waiting for Keifer Sutherland to call her.